STORIES OF
ROBOTS

Russell Punter

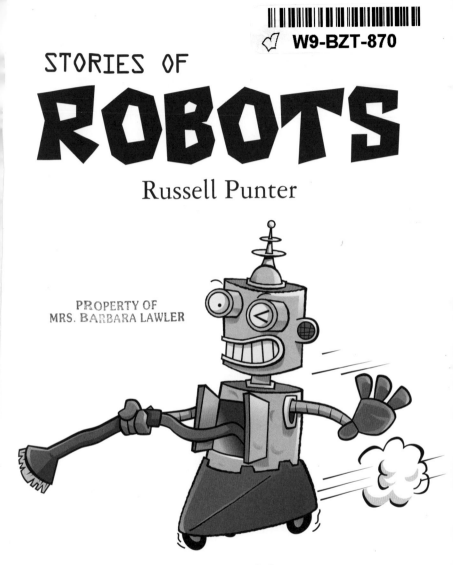

Illustrated by
Andrew Hamilton

Reading Consultant: Alison Kelly
University of Surrey Roehampton

Contents

Chapter 1

The terrible Tidybot 3

Chapter 2

Robot robbery 19

Chapter 3

Robot racers 30

Chapter 1

The terrible Tidybot

THUD!

"Luke, you're the laziest boy in the world!" cried Mrs. Lively. His room was so untidy, she could hardly get in.

3

"Look at all this mess!"
sighed Luke's mother as she
clambered over a pile of books,
clothes and toys.

"All you do all day is play
on that beeping computer,"
said Mrs. Lively, crossly.

Luke wasn't listening. He had just reached level twelve on *Android Attack.* Now he needed to concentrate.

I've had just about enough, young man!

"You have one week to clean up this room or the computer goes," threatened Mrs. Lively. "I mean it!"

Luke heard *that* loud and clear. He couldn't possibly live without his computer. But cleaning his room would take forever.

He spent the next two hours searching the Internet for cleaning companies. They were all too expensive.

Luke had almost given up hope, when an advertisement popped up on the screen.

"That's just what I need," cried Luke. "It can clean my room, then I'll send it back."

7

Just under a week later, the Tidybot arrived at Luke's house. He managed to sneak the box up to his room, before his mother dashed past on her way out.

"I want that room clean by the time I come back!" she shouted.

The front door slammed behind her. Luke had just two hours.

He ran to his room and
excitedly tore open the box.

Wow!

First, he read the instruction
booklet. Then he aimed the
remote control. The Tidybot
was ready for action.

Luke pressed a red button twice and the robot jerked to life.

ALLOW ME TO PUT AWAY YOUR CLOTHES, SIR.

In minutes, all Luke's pants, shirts and socks were off the floor and neatly put away. Luke was impressed.

He pressed button after button. The robot whizzed around the room, obeying every command.

ALLOW ME TO PUT YOUR BOOKS ON THE SHELF, SIR.

ALLOW ME TO VACUUM YOUR CARPET, SIR.

ALLOW ME TO PUT AWAY YOUR TOYS, SIR.

11

In no time at all, the bedroom was cleaner than it had ever been. Luke couldn't wait to see his mother's face when she returned.

He took a step back to admire the Tidybot's work. As he did, he heard a loud crack.

The remote control was bent and broken.

How can I return this now?

But Luke had more important things to worry about. Breaking the control unit had made the Tidybot go crazy.

ALLOW ME TO PUT AWAY YOUR BOOKS, SIR.

It hurtled around the room
until it was messier than ever.

ALLOW ME TO PUT
AWAY YOUR
CLOTHES, SIR.

Before Luke could stop it, the
rampaging robot zoomed out
of his
bedroom
and down
the stairs.

It went through every room in the house, leaving a messy trail behind.

Finally, the robot's battery went flat and it ground to a halt. Luke stared at the house in horror. What would his mother say?

He spent the next hour sweeping, mopping and polishing. Then he repacked the robot and hid it in the shed.

When he'd finished, he was so tired that he went to his bedroom to lie down. He was in for a shock.

As he slumped onto his bed in despair, his mother returned.

"Look at this room!" she cried. But Luke was so exhausted, he didn't hear.

Mrs. Lively shook her head as she carried off Luke's computer. "You really *are* the laziest boy in the world!" she said.

Chapter 2

Robot robbery

Jay C. B. was the hardest-
working robot on the building
site. He had ten different tools,
so he was always digging and
drilling.

But Jay liked the end of each day best. Only then could he switch off and recharge his battery.

Ahh. Time for a rest.

One night, as Jay was recharging, someone broke in and carried him off.

When Jay was fully charged, he awoke to find himself in a strange workshop.

A wild-haired man was fiddling with Jay's control panel.

"Who are you?" cried Jay, "and what do you want?"

"The name's Filch," snapped the man. "The rest you'll find out soon enough."

"But I should be digging back at the site," cried Jay.

"I have a much better job for you," said Filch. "I want you to dig for me... into Bullion's Bank!"

I'm not taking orders from you!

"When I've reprogramed you, you'll do whatever I want," snarled the crook.

Later that day, Filch ordered Jay to follow him to the bank.

"No!" said Jay.

Filch pushed a button on a remote control. Jay followed.

But Jay refused to dig. Filch angrily flicked two switches on his remote control.

"I obey!" said Jay, and began burrowing into the ground at top speed.

Jay kept digging... down... then across... then up...

As he burrowed along, the soil filled the narrow tunnel behind him.

I obey!

Soon Jay emerged
in Bullion's Bank.
Outside, Filch
watched Jay's
progress on a
tiny screen. He
twisted a dial
and Jay drilled
through a thick
metal door.

Filch was delighted.

"Only the electric inner door left to go," he said with a grin. "Then all the bank's gold will be mine!"

Jay's saw buzzed into action. But as it sliced through the door, an electric shock blasted Jay off his feet.

26

Suddenly, Jay felt different.
He could switch off his saw.
"I'm free!" he cried. "That
electric shock must have
stopped Filch's program."

"Now I'll fix
that no-good
crook,"
thought Jay.

Minutes later, Jay popped out of the tunnel and handed Filch two big sacks.

"Run!" he cried. "The guards saw me stealing the gold."

Filch ran home as fast as he could. But he was in for a surprise.

The greedy crook excitedly tipped out the contents of the sacks, only to to find...

Jay had filled the sacks with rubble from the tunnel.

Filch spat out a mouthful of dirt. "That's the last time I trust a robot!" he shouted.

29

Chapter 3

Robot racers

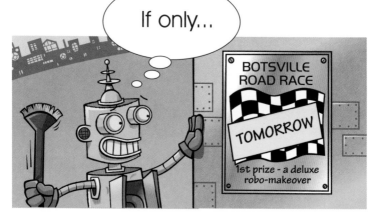

Squeaky the cleaning robot hated his job. He was out in all weather, sweeping streets. What he really wanted was to win the Botsville road race.

The winning robot would get a new memory chip and a head-to-wheel polish.

But Squeaky didn't dare enter. He was so rusty and clanky, he wasn't sure he could even finish the race.

He was feeling sorry for himself when a noisy robot zoomed past.

Tanktop was the biggest, meanest robot in town. Everyone was certain he would win tomorrow's big race.

Tanktop wasn't taking any chances. He had a plan to make sure none of the other racers even started.

That night, as the Botsville robots recharged themselves, Tanktop visited each of his rivals in secret.

He gave
Tina Turbo a
puncture...

stole Cyber
Sid's memory
chip...

undid Andi
Droid's battery
pack...

and reset
Betty Byte's
built-in
alarm clock.

She'll sleep right
through the race!

The next morning, Tanktop was the only robot at the starting line. It looked as if his plan had worked. The judge was puzzled.

It seems you're the only contestant!

I'll take my prize now!

"There must be someone else willing to race," cried the judge desperately. Tanktop was making him look stupid.

Just then a tinny voice piped up. "I will!"

Everyone in the crowd turned. "Is that Squeaky?" said someone in amazement.

You? What chance have you got?

I'd still like to try.

Squeaky's joints were feeling especially stiff today, but he couldn't miss this chance.

"Very well," said the judge, with a sigh of relief. "Robots, on your marks!"

Tanktop hadn't bothered to charge up his battery that morning. But he was confident he could still beat Squeaky.

The robots set off on their lap of the town. Tanktop raced off with a roar and Squeaky clattered off in hot pursuit.

As soon as he was out of sight of the crowd, Tanktop opened a flap in his back.

By the time Squeaky spotted the spiky trap, it was too late.

Luckily, Squeaky was so old that his wheels were made of solid rubber. They didn't burst and he was still in the race.

"I'll show that cheat!" thought Squeaky. He put on a burst of speed. Soon, he'd caught up with Tanktop.

"Let's see you get out of this!" boomed Tanktop, as he opened another compartment.

Oil!

Squeaky shut his eyes and hoped for the best, as he slithered and slid all over the road.

Woooaah!

40

CRASH!

Squeaky was left battered and dented, but at least he was still in one piece. He tried to get up and found he couldn't move. His joints were too stiff.

Now I've lost for sure!

As he sat there, Squeaky realized what he needed was all around him. Unwinding his hose, he guzzled up every last drop of oil.

Ahh! That feels good.

SLURP!

Soon, Squeaky was back on his rival's tail. Tanktop was running out of power fast.

But Tanktop still had one trick up his sleeve – his telescopic arms. He reached out to Squeaky's front wheel and undid the screw.

Sparks flew through the air as Squeaky's wheel bounced past Tanktop. In seconds, Squeaky had ground to a halt.

As the crowd came back into view, Tanktop used the last of his power to roar across the finishing line.

Tanktop was already boasting to the crowds as poor old Squeaky was carried across the line.

"Congratulations!" cried the judge as he shook Squeaky by the hand.

"Well, I suppose I almost won," Squeaky sniffed, sadly.

"Not almost," said the judge. "You *did* win. Look!"

He showed Squeaky and Tanktop the photograph taken at the finishing line.

"Your wheel crossed the line a second before Tanktop. That makes you the winner!"

Squeaky clunked with delight, the crowd cheered and Tanktop blew a fuse.

Series editor:
Lesley Sims

First published in 2004 by Usborne Publishing Ltd., Usborne House,
83-85 Saffron Hill, London EC1N 8RT, England. www.usborne.com
Copyright © 2004 Usborne Publishing Ltd.